D1085106

J
796.3
OWENS

Owens, Tom,
1960-

The Chicago Bulls
basketball team.

DATE		
JAN 17 1998		
MAR 09 1998	FEB 0 9 2007	
JUN 2 3 1998 JAN 1 2 2016		
AUG 2 9 1998		
DEC 0 1 1998		
JAN 0 2 1999		
AUG 1 7 1999		
JUL 2 3 2002		
DEC 1 6 2002		
OCT 2 1 2003		
MAY 0 3 2006		

★ *GREAT SPORTS TEAMS* ★

THE CHICAGO

BASKETBALL TEAM

Thomas S. Owens

Enslow Publishers, Inc.

44 Fadem Road	PO Box 38
Box 699	Aldershot
Springfield, NJ 07081	Hants GU12 6BP
USA	UK

Copyright © 1997 by Enslow Publishers, Inc.

Library of Congress Cataloging-in-Publication Data

Owens, Thomas S.
    The Chicago Bulls basketball team / Thomas S. Owens.
        p. cm. — (Great sports teams)
    Includes bibliographical references (p.) and index.
    Summary: Traces the history of the Windy City's basketball team, emphasizing the four championships won in the 1990s.
    ISBN 0-89490-793-X
    1. Chicago Bulls (Basketball team)—History—Juvenile literature.
    [1. Chicago Bulls (Basketball team) History. 2. Basketball—History.]
    I. Title. II. Series.
    GV885.52.C45O84 1997
    796.323'64'0977311—dc20   96-26415
                                                        CIP
                                                        AC

Printed in the United States of America

10 9 8 7 6 5 4 3 2 1

Illustration Credits: AP/Wide World Photos, pp. 4, 7, 8, 10, 13, 14, 16, 19, 20, 22, 25, 26, 28, 31, 32, 34, 37, 38.

Cover Illustration: AP/Wide World Photos.

CONTENTS

*M*ichael Jordan passes by a mob of reporters on his way to practice prior to the 1993 NBA Finals.

THREE-PEAT!

A new word needed to be invented for the Chicago Bulls. The team was a two-time NBA champion, winning consecutive titles in 1991 and 1992.

"Can the Bulls three-peat?" asked TV and radio reporters wondering if this club could win three titles in a row. Fans wondered, too, because no team had ruled the league since Boston won eight in a row from 1959 through 1966.

Two championships in a row, or an even rarer "three-peat," were dreams so big even the Bulls' future star didn't imagine them. After all, many top teams have found that injuries or attitude problems cause lost championships. Chicago's 1993 team, with a team record 67 wins in 1992, could easily have been exhausted. Attitudes could have suffered after *seven* post-season losses, but the Bulls tried to stay healthy, mentally and physically.

The Bulls charged through the first two rounds of the playoffs, eliminating Atlanta with three straight wins. In the Eastern Conference Semifinals, Chicago ousted Cleveland in four straight.

Then, when the Bulls went to New York to start the Eastern Conference Finals, everything changed. They left Madison Square Garden with two losses from the hosting Knicks—a message that their dynasty could end soon. Even the New York media seemed to gang up on the Bulls. Newspapers were filled with tales that Michael Jordan was seen gambling at an Atlantic City casino. This embarrassment was lumped atop Jordan's sore wrist and sprained ankle.

Chicago returned home to answer with teamwork, on and off the court. The entire team refused to talk to the press. When a shaken Jordan made only 3 of 18 shots in Game 3, Scottie Pippen became leading scorer with 29 points, to give the Bulls victory by a twenty-point margin. When Jordan bounced back with 54 points in Game 4, the Knicks were doomed to four straight losses.

In the NBA championship against the Charles Barkley-led Suns, the Bulls racked up two wins in two games. Game 3 took three overtimes, allowing Phoenix a 129–121 win and a stop to Chicago's hoped-for sweep.

Despite Jordan's 55 points, the Bulls struggled to edge the Suns, 111–105, in the fourth game. Phoenix countered with a 108–98 triumph, setting up a magical sixth-game finale.

The most embarrassing turnover of the series came when John Paxson moved the wrong way, and

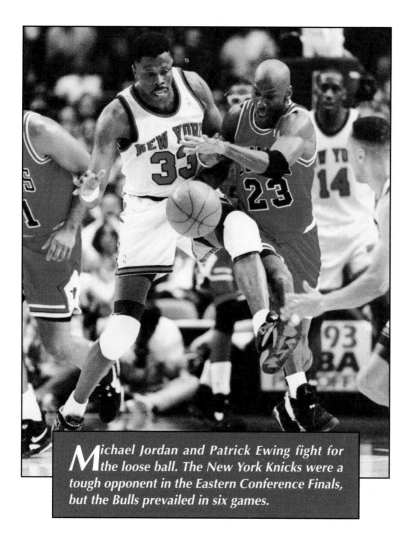

*M*ichael Jordan and Patrick Ewing fight for the loose ball. The New York Knicks were a tough opponent in the Eastern Conference Finals, but the Bulls prevailed in six games.

Pippen's intended pass squirted into the crowd. A toughened Suns defense saddled Chicago with three shot-clock turnovers. A Dan Majerle three-pointer with 5:06 left in the game gave Phoenix a lead.

Nearing the one-minute mark, the Suns were up by four, 98–94, on a layup by Kevin Johnson. Chicago's B.J. Armstrong nervously eyed the ceiling

*T*he Bulls' Horace Grant looks to block the shot of Charles Barkley. Barkley and the Phoenix Suns played hard, but Chicago beat the Suns and won their third straight championship.

scoreboard. Jordan hugged Armstrong from behind, whispering words of hope in his ear.

The hope must have haunted Phoenix's Frank Johnson, who missed a jumper with forty-three seconds left. Jordan snagged a rebound, then cruised end to end through a crowded court, going "coast to coast." His trademark, a flying layup, complete with ball palmed firmly, cut the Suns' lead to 98–96.

Could Phoenix ice the win, demanding a seventh game? Majerle failed to put the game out of reach when his baseliner fell short, missing the hoop and just grazing the net. A Pippen rebound readied the Bulls for their final stampede, with only 14.1 seconds remaining.

Across midcourt, Jordan passed to Pippen. In a surprise move, Pippen went to Grant. The cold-shooting Grant then picked an unlikely hero, passing to Paxson. "Pax" canned a three-pointer, bringing a "three-peat" and a 99–98 win. Grant topped his assist with yet another smooth move to save the victory. Kevin Johnson handled Phoenix's last hope. However, KJ saw his jump shot die quickly, when Grant slapped the ball out of Johnson's hands.

Two key plays by Grant in the final seconds weren't the only surprises for happy Bulls fans. The biggest shock was that the winning basket produced the first Chicago points of the quarter scored by someone other than Jordan.

Jordan averaged 41 points per game in the championship, one of four records he set against the Suns.

The city of Chicago set some records in celebrating the Bulls' third title. Signs hanging in downtown Chicago streets made another new word for the team's championship dictionary: "Three-mendous!" Another banner used the same short and sweet language to describe the team with three straight championships:

"Trip-Bulls!"

*B*oxing out their opponents, Tom Boerwinkle and Jerry Sloan corral the rebound. In the Bull's first season they set a record for victories by a first-year expansion team.

CHICAGO BASKETBALL

Long before the Bulls, professional basketball was a part of Chicago. In fact, pro hoops have been part of The Windy City off and on since 1925. Two clubs (both called the Bruins) were started by George "Papa Bear" Halas, founder and coach of the Chicago Bears football team. Another early Chicago team from the 1920s would later be known as the Harlem Globetrotters. They began playing all road games when the skating rink where they played closed down.

Chicago's first NBA team, the Stags, lasted only from 1946 to 1950. Ten years later, Chicago's next NBA entry, the Packers, lasted only two seasons. Windy City fans seemed content with Bears football, Black Hawks hockey, or baseball from the Cubs or the decades-old White Sox.

The Bulls were born in 1966. Dick Klein headed a group of investors who joined the NBA for $1.25 million.

Before the club's final naming, Klein considered calling it the Matadors or Conquistadors, because the team played in the Amphitheater near the Chicago livestock yards. He finally settled on the Bulls.

Klein dubbed the costumed team mascot Benny the Bull, after Ben Bentley, the first dramatic public address announcer to introduce Bulls players before games. Bentley wondered if he'd be expected to dress up in the Bulls costume.[1]

The first season ended with a 33–48 record, earning the Bulls fourth place and a playoff spot. They set a record for victories by a first-year expansion team. After only one more season, Johnny "Red" Kerr was named NBA Coach of the Year. Then Kerr quit to lead the new expansion team in Phoenix, following many arguments with Bulls owner Klein.

Dick Motta began an eight-year stay as coach in 1968–69. A trade with the new Milwaukee Bucks landed Bob Love, who went on to lead the team in scoring for seven straight seasons.

By 1974–75, the Bulls were Midwest Division champions. For the next five years, they were constant contenders, but never full-time winners.

Even when Michael Jordan debuted with the Bulls in 1984–85, the team finished with a 38–44 mark. The Bulls dipped to 30–52 when Jordan broke his foot in 1985. It wasn't until 1987–88—when Phil Jackson joined the team as an assistant coach—that the Bulls topped fifty wins for the first time since 1974.

Jackson took over as head coach in 1989–90, and the Bulls won a then-record 55 games. The following

Determined to score, the Bulls' Jerry Sloan slides a reverse lay-up underneath Bucks' center Kareem Abdul-Jabbar. By 1974–75 the Bulls had become Midwest Division Champions.

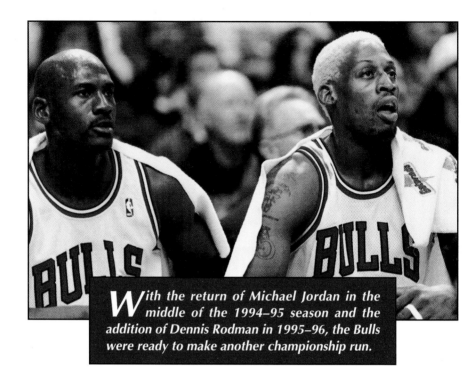

With the return of Michael Jordan in the middle of the 1994–95 season and the addition of Dennis Rodman in 1995–96, the Bulls were ready to make another championship run.

year, the team earned its first of three straight championships. As defending champs in 1991–92, the Bulls climbed to a best-ever 67–15 record, the third best in NBA history.

In 1993, the Bulls became the third team in NBA history to "three-peat," earning a third straight title. Then the unthinkable happened. On October 6, 1993, Michael Jordan retired to join another Chicago sports team, the Chicago White Sox, to play minor-league baseball.

Without Jordan, Scottie Pippen's 22 points per game led the Bulls in 1993–94. He was aided by Toni Kukoc, a six-foot-eleven-inch player from Croatia who was considered the best player in Europe at the time. The Knicks still eliminated the Bulls' quest for a fourth straight title in a seventh-game showdown in the conference semifinals.

Jordan returned to basketball on March 18, 1995, attracting a record 24,247 fans. It was too late to save the season, though. The Bulls were eliminated by the Orlando Magic in the conference semifinals. It was the Bulls' last game in Chicago Stadium. A new facility was already being built across Madison Street. The United Center hosted its first NBA game on November 4, 1994, as the Bulls beat Charlotte, 89–83.

Chicago's 1995–96 season brought 72 wins and only 10 losses, rewriting basketball history on the way to another championship. Celebrating their thirtieth anniversary in the NBA, the Bulls threatened to remain the league's powerhouse into a new century.

*S*cottie Pippen goes up for the shot against Shawn Kemp (40) and Frank Brickowski (34) of the Seattle SuperSonics. In 1993–94, Pippen led the Bulls in points, rebounds, assists, steals, and blocks.

STAR BULLS

Although Michael Jordan is one of Chicago's brightest stars, there are other Bulls players who have been guiding lights for their team.

Scottie Pippen

Growing up in Hamburg, Arkansas, in a family of a dozen children, Scottie Pippen didn't have to look hard for basketball teammates or opponents. But the six-foot, 150-pound Pippen worked as his high school's football team manager. Scottie's hoop dreams appeared later, when he grew to his current six feet seven inches and 210 pounds.

Pippen excelled as Jordan's offensive counterpart during 1992–93, and his team record of 317 consecutive games played peaked that season. He was second in fan balloting as an all-star starter, behind only Jordan. Fans recognized that Jordan wouldn't lead the league in scoring without Pippen, the team's annual assist leader.

When Jordan left before the 1993–94 season, Pippen paced the Bulls with a career-high 22 points per game, and topped the team in minutes played, rebounds, assists, steals, and blocked shots. The last player to lead a team in points, rebounds, assists, steals, and blocked shots was Dave Cowens of the Boston Celtics, in the 1977–78 season. Pippen earned the All-Star Game Most Valuable Player award, leading all players with 29 points, 11 rebounds, and 4 steals.

Jerry Sloan

Jerry joined the Bull's first team in 1966. He was so popular that the team played five games in Evansville to make the most of Sloan's Illinois fame. Johnny Kerr, his first Bulls coach, remembered that "I called him 'road hog,' because when the opposing guard brought the ball up the court, Sloan would meet him at the half-court line and body the guy."[1] This skill gained Sloan spots on four NBA all-defensive first teams. Players from other teams called Sloan "The Human Chainsaw," after he sliced through opposing defenses.

Sloan retired in 1976, and became the first Bulls player to have his jersey number (4) retired. He had played in 696 games, a team record. Sloan returned to coach the Bulls in 1979, leading his old team to two consecutive playoff appearances. He became head coach of the Utah Jazz in 1988.

*B*ob Love receives a commemorative ring from Bulls' Vice President of Basketball Operations Jerry Krause after having his number retired on January 14, 1994.

When Jerry Krause became Chicago's general manager in 1985, he said, "I wish I could get 12 players just like Jerry Sloan, but that's impossible."[2]

Bob Love

On November 7, 1968, the Milwaukee Bucks traded Bob Weiss and a skinny substitute, Bob "Butterbean" Love, to Chicago. A "throw-in" to seal the deal, Love was young and thin, not the typical hardwood warrior, but during his first full season with the Bulls in 1969–70, Butterbean became the team's leading scorer, with 21 points per game. Teammates copied his success, setting an all-time team record with 9,423 points scored.

Michael Jordan finishes the play by slamming the ball with authority. Many people feel that Michael Jordan is the best basketball player in history.

A season later, Love owned team records for points scored (2,043) and minutes played (3,482) that would be unbroken until Michael Jordan's arrival. A Chicago ironman, Love led the team in minutes played for four seasons running.

By the time Love left in a 1976 trade with the Knicks, he was the Bulls' all-time scoring leader (12,623), and he held four other offensive career records. Eight of his eleven seasons in the NBA were spent as a Bull. His jersey number (10) was retired on January 14, 1994.

The Chicago Bulls Basketball Team

Michael Jordan

Beginning with his 1984 NBA debut, Michael Jordan excited fans everywhere with high-voltage play. In 1985, he told reporters, "My ultimate goal is to help bring a championship to Chicago. I know people laugh and say it will never happen, but it would be a bit foolish to bet against it."[3] Three championships later, Jordan broke the hearts of millions of fans. On October 6, 1993, he announced he was retiring. He said he'd like to play pro baseball.

Playing for the White Sox' minor-league double-A team in Birmingham, Alabama, Jordan hit only .202. His 88 hits were outnumbered by 112 strikeouts. In right field, he made 11 errors.

Because Jordan thought baseball's 1994–95 strike was halting his progress in the new sport, he returned to the Bulls, wearing number 45, because his first number (23) had been retired.

During the Bulls' historic 72–10 season in 1995–96, Jordan started every game and averaged 30.4 points per outing on the way to his fourth MVP award and record eighth scoring title. In the postseason, Jordan led the Bulls to their fourth NBA Championship.

Who will the next great Bulls be? Players who, like these players, show more than talent. Pippen, Sloan, and Love, and, of course, Jordan, tried their hardest, and never gave up. That's what makes good players into great players.

*P*hil Jackson is only the ninth person to win a championship as both a player and coach.

LEADING THE BULLS

No team succeeds with talented players alone. Some of the finest Bulls teams in history have succeeded due to talent off the court. Coaches and owners can make a big difference.

Here are some of the many behind-the-scenes stars in Chicago hoop history.

Phil Jackson

As a six-foot eight-inch teenager growing up in Montana, Jackson boasted that he could sit in the backseat of a car and open both doors at once. [1]

As a player, Jackson started his thirteen-year career in 1968 with a spot on the NBA All-Rookie Team, and finished with two seasons for the New Jersey Nets. Before joining the Bulls as an assistant coach in 1987, Jax was a head coach for the Albany Patroons in the Continental Basketball Association for five seasons.

As skipper of the 1991 champs, Jackson became only the ninth man in NBA history to be part of a championship team both as a player (1973 Knicks) and a coach. Never before had a new NBA coach reached 200 career wins so quickly.

Jerry Reinsdorf

The chairman of the Bulls was born in Brooklyn in 1936, but has lived in Chicago since 1957. The former Knicks fan led the group that purchased the Bulls on March 13, 1985. Previously, the team had lost money yearly, and some sportswriters feared new Bulls owners would move to a new, more profitable city. Instead, Reinsdorf pushed attendance sky high by hiring the team's first group of season-ticket sellers. He led the effort to build a new stadium for the team.

By taking an interest in the daily success of the team on and off the court, Reinsdorf did more than build a winner. The Bulls were valued at a mere $14.8 million before being sold. By the time of the first championship, the club's worth was more than $100 million.

Jerry Krause

Only thirteen days after acquiring the Bulls, Reinsdorf hired Chicagoan Krause as vice president of basketball operations. The owner's wealth and patience combined perfectly with Krause's courtside knowledge.

Krause's early career included more than thirty years of scouting for basketball and baseball teams,

*B*ulls owner Jerry Reinsdorf (left) is one of the men most responsible for the Bulls' success. Reinsdorf has seen the franchise grow from being worth $14.8 million to over $100 million today.

including Reinsdorf's White Sox. Krause's current job puts him in charge of judging players, coaches, and scouts—the whole team—helping decide who stays and who goes.

Just how much did Krause mold the Bulls into one of history's greatest teams? By the time of the third championship, the entire roster of players and coaches, except for Jordan, were Krause-made discoveries. When players and staff stood together after the sixth game of the 1995–96 NBA championship to accept their trophy, owner Reinsdorf asked the crowd to salute Krause, the man who brought it all together.

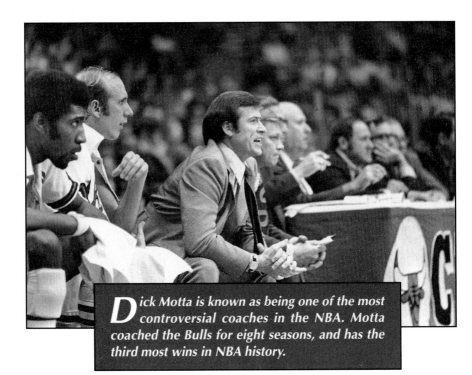

Dick Motta is known as being one of the most controversial coaches in the NBA. Motta coached the Bulls for eight seasons, and has the third most wins in NBA history.

Tex Winter

The first year Krause was hired, he asked for Winter's help as a consultant and assistant coach. Winter had spent nearly forty years as a coach in college and pro ball, starting as an assistant at Kansas State in 1947.

When Jackson became head coach, he made Assistant Coach Winter an unlikely star. Winter was allowed to overhaul all the Bulls' offensive plans.

Winter had spent decades with college teams perfecting the triangle, a triple-post offense that allowed lots of ball movement between all five starters. Passing, teamwork, and sharing would make the offense a

The Chicago Bulls Basketball Team

hit, Jackson felt. The head coach knew that this system was unknown to many teams, and that his Bulls tended to stand back and wait for Jordan to score. Turning the offense over to Winter was one of Jackson's first brainstorms.

Dick Motta

One of the first great head coaches in Bulls history had an unusual past. At five feet ten inches, he never played basketball himself at his Utah high school, or while attending Utah State University. When he assumed leadership of the Bulls in 1968, Motta's experience was limited to six years of small-college coaching.

Still, crowds started coming to see Motta coach. Although Motta filled the Bulls with enthusiasm, he was known to explode during games. Once, he was fined $1,500 for spitting on the ball and handing it back to a referee in protest. Once, an opposing coach received a technical because of Motta's antics. Why? The rival coach couldn't believe that neither referee caught Motta drop-kicking the basketball into the upper deck of the arena, and protested too much.

Despite taking teams to the playoffs for six straight years, Motta was fired after finishing fourth with a 24-58 record in 1976.

Michael Jordan and Scottie Pippen have been the two main players on each of the Chicago Bulls' championship teams.

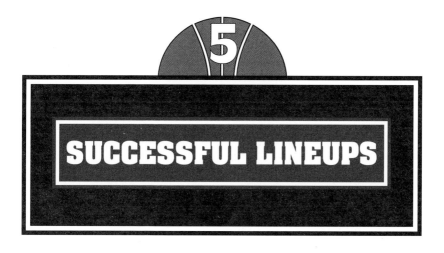

SUCCESSFUL LINEUPS

Although the Bulls were world champions for three years straight, the teams were not exact copies of each other. Sure, Michael Jordan and Scottie Pippen were the core of each club's success. Yet, each year, the Bulls found first place in a different way.

The 1990–91 Lineup

The first Bulls championship in 1991 didn't surprise the world. After all, the team had won 55 games a year earlier, not getting eliminated until the seventh game of the Eastern Conference Finals by eventual champion Detroit.

When the future champions beat Phoenix, 155–127, on December 4, 1990, a new record was set for the most points ever scored in regulation. On December 15, the Bulls held Cleveland to only five first-quarter points on the way to a win.

Head coach Phil Jackson was in charge for only his second year in 1991. This time, the Bulls turned the tables on rival Detroit in the Eastern Conference Finals, sweeping the Pistons in four straight. Detroit pouted afterward, stomping off the Bull's home floor without congratulating the winners.

When the Bulls claimed the championship in five games against the Lakers, what happened after the final 108–101 win was, to some fans, as memorable as the game itself. TV cameras showed reserve guard Craig Hodges leading the team in prayer. The seldom-seen substitute sparkled during the 1991 All-Star weekend, winning his second consecutive three-point title by sinking 19 consecutive shots.

Following a fourth straight Finals win against the Lakers, Michael Jordan was seen seated by his father in the locker room, holding the championship trophy and weeping. Seven years of waiting for the title had marked Jordan's career. The Bulls had waited a quarter century.

Part of the Bulls' first-title secret was consistency. In 1991, Jordan, Pippen, B. J. Armstrong, and John Paxson played in every regular-season game.

The 1991–92 Lineup

This Bulls squad won 67 games. Along with 31 straight road games, they reeled off a fourteen-game winning streak, for two more team records.

To defend their title in 1992, the Bulls made only a few changes. Horace Grant, who had shared his rookie season with Pippen back in 1987, reached a career-high

*M*ichael Jordan is overcome with emotion after the Bulls beat the Los Angeles Lakers for their first-ever NBA Championship. The Bulls had waited twenty-five years for their first title.

scoring average (14.2 points per game). Reserve Dennis Hopson was replaced on the roster by Bobby Hansen.

The new Bull's part-time play was highlighted by a clutch performance in the deciding sixth game of the NBA Finals against Portland. After the third quarter, the Trailblazers led by 15 points. Jackson began the fourth with Hansen and three other new faces in the lineup. Hansen's immediate steal and three-point basket began the comeback, leading to the Bulls'

*H*orace Grant was one of the main contributors to the Bulls' three straight championships. After the 1993–94 season, Grant left to join the Orlando Magic.

clinching another championship. Hansen was one of the Bulls who returned to dance on the scorer's table, hoist the trophy in the air, and celebrate with Chicago fans after winning the final game.

What feat could compete with the clinching comeback? Jordan poured in 56 third-game points to guarantee a first-round playoff sweep against the Miami Heat, setting the stage for a dramatic postseason.

The 1992-93 Lineup

The Bulls began their third title chase filled with worry. They boosted their P. J. (Pippen and Jordan)

The Chicago Bulls Basketball Team

output with a strong supporting cast. Armstrong took over for the creaky-kneed Paxson and became the league's top three-point shooter, succeeding more than 45 percent of the time (63 for 139). The guard was the only Bull to play in all eighty-two regular-season games. Grant came through with another season past the thousand-point horizon.

Hansen wasn't re-signed, but part-timer Scott Williams scored more points in 1992–93 than in the two prior years together. Newcomers Trent Tucker and Rodney McCray added more bench strength, with Tucker sinking a team-record 6 consecutive three-point baskets in one game against Atlanta.

The Bulls dropped to a 57–25 record, down from their other championship seasons. Pippen and Jordan had begun the season with little rest, spending the summer of 1992 with the U.S. Olympic "Dream Team." Armstrong was the only starting Bull to remain free of injuries.

The tired Bulls had fewer dazzling moments, but kept building lifetime milestones. Jackson set a coaching record, getting a 200th career win faster than any other coach. Jordan's 20,000th career point came on January 8, after only 620 games. Only Wilt Chamberlain earned the point level faster.

For years, fans may study the makeup of those three championship Bulls teams. The highest score may decide a game's outcome, but deciding which players make the perfect team is the biggest challenge.

*T*he Bulls started the 1994–95 season with a new home, The United Center (center), which could hold almost 3,000 more people than the Bulls' previous home, Chicago Stadium, (right).

A WINNING TRADITION

True fans always love their team, even without a championship. Consider this: The Bulls ended the 1995–96 season with a streak of 427 straight sellouts. (That is, they sold out every game for more than five and a half years.) Their logo appears on clothing worldwide. In fact, estimates say that more than a third of all NBA souvenirs are Bulls related.

The team made the United Center its new home in 1994, boasting the NBA's second biggest arena with 21,500 seats. This arena was nearly three thousand seats larger than the Bulls' previous home, Chicago Stadium. For Michael Jordan's first home game return in 1995, United Center was packed with 24,247 fans. The Bulls do more than play hard to get big crowds. To help ticket sales, the team plans more than thirty promotions yearly for home games, giving away posters, hats, or other souvenirs to fans who attend.

Because nearly thirty people share ownership of the Bulls, they have many sources of steady money. Combining owner monies with huge income from ticket sales, TV and radio appearances, and souvenirs, the Bulls should have cash for years to come. Being one of the league's richest teams means that the Bulls will have the dollars to hire the best free agents, while paying enough to keep their finest talent.

Even after the Bulls' one-two scoring punch of Jordan and Scottie Pippen depart, the club has a bright future. The Bulls have created the same team tradition that baseball's New York Yankees have enjoyed. Win or lose, players are proud to be part of the organization.

Part of that pride comes from knowing that a Bull can be a Bull forever. Remember John Paxson, the nine-year guard, and Johnny "Red" Kerr, the team's first-ever coach? Both found new jobs with the team off the court, Kerr as an announcer and Paxson as an assistant coach. Bob Love, after eight years as a Bulls star, was hired to make speeches in the Chicago community and spread fan support for the team.

Players aren't the only talented members of the Bulls. As long as the team keeps smart people like Coach Phil Jackson and General Manager Jerry Krause around, the right mix of athletes can be found.

Jackson and Krause showed how they can keep a winner winning by trading Will Perdue to San Antonio for Dennis Rodman before the start of the 1995–96 season. Rodman was hated by Chicago fans as one of the Detroit Pistons' "Bad Boys," who pushed and elbowed the Bulls while winning the 1989 and 1990

*T*he celebration begins after time runs out in Game 6 of the 1996 NBA Finals. The Bulls beat the Seattle SuperSonics by the score of 87–75.

Eastern Conference Finals. Since then, he has confused fans everywhere by showing off two tattooed arms, painted fingernails, and wildly colored hair.

Nevertheless, Rodman remained one of the top rebounders and defensive stars of the 1990s. Despite his unusual personality, the Bulls knew he could bring more wins.

The Bulls are famous for seeking talent anywhere. They've used the lesser-known Continental Basketball Association, where Jackson once coached, to find worthy players to fill in for injured Bulls, signing some substitutes for only ten days at a time.

Also, Chicago scours small colleges, considers the unwanted players from other teams, and even patrols

D*ennis Rodman celebrates after scoring against the New York Knicks. Rodman came to the Bulls in a trade with the San Antonio Spurs for Will Perdue.*

other countries. After discovering Croatia's Toni Kukoc in 1990, the Bulls hired Ivica Dukan as their first supervisor of European scouting. Dukan had played fourteen years in England, Switzerland, France, and Yugoslavia.

Bulls fans shouldn't worry if their team suffers through a losing season or two. NBA rules are in their favor. The worst-record teams from the previous season get the first choices in the following college draft. Thanks to a 27–55, fifth-place record in 1984, the Bulls were allowed the third pick of the first round, bringing in Michael Jordan.

Jordan, Coach Jackson, and Kukoc were major forces as the Bulls overpowered the Seattle Supersonics in six games to win the 1995–96 championship. Kukoc was named the NBA's Sixth Man for the season, for being a useful substitute. His supersubbing for the injured Pippen in the finals proved why he won the award.

Although public worry began immediately over whether the coach and Jordan would remain for long with Chicago, loyal fans knew that history was on the Bull's side. Just like Kukoc's, new faces will always be there to help the Bulls keep chasing championships for years to come.

STATISTICS

Team Record

SEASON	SEASON RECORD	PLAYOFF RECORD	COACH	DIVISION FINISH
1966–67	33-48	0-3	John Kerr	4th
1967–68	29-53	1-4	John Kerr	4th
1968–69	33-49	—	Dick Motta	5th
1969–70	39-43	1-4	Dick Motta	3rd
1970–71	51-31	3-4	Dick Motta	2nd
1971–72	57-25	0-4	Dick Motta	2nd
1972–73	51-31	3-4	Dick Motta	2nd
1973–74	54-28	4-7	Dick Motta	2nd
1974–75	47-35	7-6	Dick Motta	1st
1975–76	24-58	—	Dick Motta	4th
1976–77	44-38	1-2	Ed Badger	2nd
1977–78	40-42	—	Ed Badger	3rd
1978–79	31-51	—	Larry Costello/ Scotty Robertson	5th
1979–80	30-52	—	Jerry Sloan	4th
1980–81	45-37	2-4	Jerry Sloan	2nd
1981–82	34-48	—	Jerry Sloan/ Rod Thorn	5th
1982–83	28-54	—	Paul Westhead	4th
1983–84	27-55	—	Kevin Loughery	5th
1984–85	38-44	1-3	Kevin Loughery	3rd
1985–86	30-52	0-3	Stan Albeck	4th
1986–87	40-42	0-3	Doug Collins	5th
1987–88	50-32	4-6	Doug Collins	2nd
1988–89	47-35	9-8	Doug Collins	5th
1989–90	55-27	10-6	Phil Jackson	2nd
1990–91	61-21	15-2	Phil Jackson	1st

Team Record (con't)

SEASON	SEASON RECORD	PLAYOFF RECORD	COACH	DIVISION FINISH
1991–92	67-15	15-7	Phil Jackson	1st
1992–93	57-25	15-4	Phil Jackson	1st
1993–94	55-27	6-4	Phil Jackson	2nd
1994–95	47-35	5-5	Phil Jackson	3rd
1995–96	72-10	15-3	Phil Jackson	1st
Totals	1316-1143	117-96		

Coaching Records

COACH	YEARS COACHED	RECORD	CHAMPIONSHIPS
John Kerr	1966–68	62-101	None
Dick Motta	1968–76	356-300	1974–75 Midwest Division (tie)
Ed Badger	1976–78	84-80	None
Larry Costello	1978–79	20-36	None
Scotty Robertson	1978–79	11-15	None
Jerry Sloan	1979–82	94-122	None
Rod Thorn	1981–82	15-15	None
Paul Westhead	1982–83	28-54	None
Kevin Loughery	1983–85	65-99	None
Stan Albeck	1985–86	30-52	None
Doug Collins	1986–89	137-109	None
Phil Jackson	1989–	414-160	NBA Champions, 1990–91, 1991–92 1992–93, 1995–96

Ten Greatest Bulls

					CAREER STATISTICS					
PLAYER	**SEA**	**YRS**	**G**	**REB**	**AST**	**BLK**	**STL**	**PTS**	**AVG**
Tom Boerwinkle	1968–78	10	635	5,745	2,007	—	—	4,596	7.2
Artis Gilmore	1976–82	12	909	9,161	1,777	1,747	470	15,579	17.1
Horace Grant	1987–94	9	683	6,016	1,659	741	725	8,661	12.7
Michael Jordan	1984–93, 1994–	11	766	4,879	4,377	739	2,025	24,489	32.0
Bob Love	1968–76	11	789	4,653	1,123	—	—	13,895	17.6
Scottie Pippen	1987–	9	707	4,900	3,723	677	1,538	12,490	17.7
Jerry Sloan	1966–76	11	755	5,615	1,925	—	—	10,571	14.0
Reggie Theus	1978–84	13	1,026	3,349	6,453	236	1,206	19,015	18.5
Norm Van Lier	1971–78	10	746	3,596	5,217	—	—	8,770	11.8
Chet Walker	1969–75	13	1,032	7,314	2,126	—	—	18,831	18.2

SEA=Seasons with Bulls   REB=Rebounds   STL=Steals
YRS=Years in the NBA   AST=Assists   PTS=Total Points
G=Games   BLK=Blocks   AVG=Scoring Average

The Chicago Bulls Basketball Team

CHAPTER NOTES

Chapter 2

1. Roland Lazenby, *And Now, Your Chicago Bulls! A 30-Year Celebration* (Dallas: Taylor Publishing, 1995), p. 44.

Chapter 3

1. Johnny Kerr and Terry Pluto, *Bull Session* (Chicago: Bonus Books, 1989), p. 53.

2. Tom Owens, "Pre-Michael Incredi-Bull Stars," *Pakrat's Magazine,* vol. 2, no. 1, January 1995, p. 18.

3. George Beahm, *Michael Jordan: A Shooting Star* (Kansas City, Mo.: Andrews and McMeel, 1994) p. 130.

Chapter 4

1. Phil Jackson and Hugh Delahanty, *Sacred Hoops: The Spiritual Lessons of a Hardwood Warrior* (New York: Hyperion Publishing, 1995), p. 30.

GLOSSARY

assist—The action (as a throw or pass) of a player who enables a teammate to score a goal.

baseliner—A shot taken by a player who is close to the baseline on either side of the basket. The baseline is the out-of-bounds marker underneath each basket.

center—Also known as the five man; usually a team's tallest and strongest player. The actions of the guards and forwards revolve around trying to get the ball to the center for easy inside shots.

dynasty—A team that has dominated its sport for a long period of time.

hardwood—The basketball court or playing surface.

jumper—A shot taken after a player has jumped straight up in the air; also known as a jump shot.

layup—A shot that comes from about three-feet from the basket, or closer. The player, usually after a drive or just playing under the basket, flips the ball up and into the net, sometimes banking it off the backboard.

NBA—National Basketball Association.

playoffs—The system that matches the NBA teams with the best records each year in a series of games to determine the champion.

point guard—Often referred to as the one guard. This is the player who leads the offense and does most of the ball handling.

power forward—This position is also known as the four. The power forward is counted on for defense, rebounding, and some inside scoring.

powerhouse—A team that has a group of players who are capable of winning every game.

rebound—The retrieving of a ball after a missed shot.

The Chicago Bulls Basketball Team

shooting guard—Also known as the two guard. This player is often counted on for outside shooting, especially three-point shooting.

skipper—The manager or head coach of the team.

small forward—Also called the three man. These players are usually counted on for both outside and inside scoring, as well as playing good perimeter defense.

steal—This occurs when one player is able to take the ball away from the opposing team.

sweep—This occurs when a team wins every game of any given playoff series.

three-peat—When one team wins the championship three years in a row.

three-pointer—A shot that comes from beyond the three-point line, twenty-two feet or further from the basket.

triangle offense—Offensive system designed by Tex Winter that emphasizes moving the ball among all five of the players on the court at that time.

turnover—The act of a team losing possession of the ball as a result of an error or rules violation.

FURTHER READING

Aaseng, Nathan. *Sports Great Michael Jordan.* Springfield, N.J.: Enslow Publishers, 1992.

Beahm, George. *Michael Jordan: A Shooting Star.* Kansas City, Mo.: Andrews and McNeel, 1994.

Bjarkman, Peter. *Sports Great Scottie Pippen.* Springfield, N.J.: Enslow Publishers, 1996.

Jackson, Phil and Hugh Delanty. *Sacred Hoops: Spiritual Lessons of a Hardwood Warrior.* New York: Hyperion, 1995.

Jackson, Phil, and Charles Rosen. *Maverick: More than a Game.* Chicago: Playboy Press, 1975.

Kerr, Johnny, and Terry Pluto. *Bull Session.* Chicago: Bonus Books, 1989.

Knapp, Ron. *Michael Jordan: Star Guard.* Springfield, N.J.: Enslow Publishers, 1994.

Kornbluth, Jesse. *Airborne: The Triumph and Struggle of Michael Jordan.* Old Tappan, N.J.: Macmillan Books, 1995.

Lablanc, Michael. *Professional Sports Team Histories: National Basketball Association.* Detroit: Gale Publications, 1994.

Lazenby, Roland. *And Now, Your Chicago Bulls! A 30-Year Celebration.* Dallas: Taylor Publishing, 1995.

Naughton, Jim. *Taking to the Air: The Rise of Michael Jordan.* New York: Warner Books, 1992.

1995–1996 Chicago Bulls Media Guide.

1994–1995 Chicago Bulls Media Guide.

Smith, Sam. *The Jordan Rules.* New York: Simon & Schuster, 1992.

Thornley, Stew. *Sports Great Dennis Rodman.* Springfield, N.J.: Enslow Publishers, 1996.

Three-peat! Chicago: Tribune Publishing, 1993.

INDEX

WHERE TO WRITE

Chicago Bulls
United Center
1901 W. Madison St.
Chicago, IL 60612

WEBSITE

http://www.nba.com/bulls/